Praise for *Stand* and *The Way of Becoming*

Stand is profound! With her raw honesty and vulnerability, Kerry shows us how to navigate life's darkest valleys. Each page echoes with the assurance that God's presence is woven into every trial, and His promises remain unshaken. *Stand* will inspire, equip, and embolden you to face life's hardest battles with God's eternal hope.

JEANNE CELESTINE LAKIN, Human Rights Advocate, Author, *A Voice in the Darkness: Memoir of a Rwandan Genocide Survivor*

I have long dreamt of bottling Kerry's words so others could benefit from her marvelous mind and mentorship, just as Moriah and I have. I can now truly say, "Dream Realized!" *The Way of Becoming* is a beautiful work that does just that. Consider her insights "bottled" and ready for the drinking.

JOEL SMALLBONE, 4x Grammy Award Winning Artist, for KING + COUNTRY, Actor, Director, *Unsung Hero*

It's rare to find an individual who combines spectacularly sharp intellect with a beautifully softened heart. Kerry is one of those rarities. *The Way of Becoming* is simply brilliant! Its brilliance stems not from Kerry's exceptional talent but from what God carried her through and revealed to her. The candid narrative, the divine teachings, and the profound tools of encouragement are a must-read for a generation stuck on their journey toward the Divine.

MARK STUART, 2x Grammy Award Winning Artist, Audio Adrenaline, Author, *Losing My Voice to Find It*

Kerry's ability to communicate through writing, speaking, and interacting with people from all walks of life is a generational gift to the world. Her boldness to live out her faith no matter the season or environment has been one of the greatest encouragements of the 20+ years I've known her. It gives me great joy knowing *The Way of Becoming* will impact people across the globe just as it has impacted me. Kerry is one of the strongest, most enduring humans I have ever known, and if I had even an ounce of her endurance, I would win every race on the planet.

SALLY MCRAE, Professional Ultra-Mountain Runner, Speaker, and Author, *Choose Strong*

Kerry has always been an engaging storyteller and a fantastic public speaker, but her book shows she is an equally great writer, which is rare. What sets Kerry apart most, however, is how her stories and insights consistently change people for the better.

DR. MARTY MAKARY, Surgeon, Public Policy Expert, and 3x *New York Times* Bestselling Author, *Unaccountable*, *The Price We Pay*, and *Blind Spots*

The Way of Becoming brings us twelve faith practices based on Scripture yet outside any particular church denomination. Kerry wants to give people what God has given her so that they, too, can grow and get unstuck by applying them to their lives. I certainly have.

MELODEE DEVEVO, Singer and Violinist, Grammy Award Winner, Casting Crowns

Kerry has gone against the grain of culture to craft the art of soul-sorting for leaders. Using the tools from *The Way of Becoming*, I can guide my career and colleagues with a sound mind and open heart. I'm so thankful her research is finally in sharable form so I can gift the gold in these pages to those I love most.

MORIAH SMALLBONE, MŌRIAH, Artist, Actress, and Producer

Stand is captivating—breathtaking. Yet, it is only one of the beautiful gems from Kerry's book, *The Way of Becoming* . . . masterfully pieced together from her life stories interwoven with God's Word, and revealing how we can press into the Lord in those painful seasons we all face.

MARIA JACOBY, DC Ambassador for Mama Maggie's Ministry, Stephen's Children, Egypt

Kerry's tools have helped me connect my faith with my background as a psychologist. In just one afternoon of using the tools during a personal crisis I was saved hours of therapy. Kerry's soul-sorting method proved the best crisis counseling I have ever had. *The Way of Becoming* is a gift that can help transform you if you are ready to dive in and do the work.

DR. KATHY ZAKARIAN, Licensed Clinical Psychologist, 20+ years in college counseling.

Kerry's writing is wonderful, and her heart so deep. Of course, they go together. Her analysis reveals the opportunity for a new life to take root—a contemplative life, a life of intentionally practicing the presence of God, which is indeed the beauty for ashes.

HYATT MOORE, Painter, Author, and Former CEO, Wycliffe Bible Translators

When I heard Kerry speak at a women's retreat, God's presence was palpable. Her unique voice weaves together her experiences of miracles and pain, telling God's timeless story and creating space for others to encounter God's presence. When Kerry shared a preview of this book with me, I expected to be disappointed: how could the power and beauty of this very personal, interactive content possibly transfer into compelling print? My eyes welled with tears to discover it does. In a world of bookshelves filled with Christian self-help and intellectual depictions of who God is and what He wants, *The Way of Becoming* will wash over readers like cleansing water. It vibrates with tested authenticity and offers a simple, freeing framework for *how* to meet God in our broken places and build wholeness-growing lives.

LYDIA VOGT, Strategy and Execution Senior Lead, International Justice Mission

This beautiful and eminently practical book is a treasure. Kerry writes with the urgency, sensitivity, and clarity of a heart undone by the deep things of God. She is a true friend of Jesus, and her words speak of a lifetime spent cultivating His presence and walking in His love and wisdom.

AKHTAR SHAH AND SARAH BELCHER, The Foundry, Kingdom Embassy, U.K.

As a relational therapist, I engage in the broken areas and unresolved hurts people bring into my office. The twelve tools in *The Way of Becoming* are compatible with any age, intellect, denomination, ethnicity, and spiritual maturity, offering daily practices that bring people into God's design for wholeness, purpose, and freedom in Christ.

LORI SANNER, LPC, Marriage and Family Counselor

Kerry weaves a tapestry of the transcendent faithfulness of our Abba Father in the ordinary sufferings and joys of life, inviting the reader to make prayer a continual conversation with Jesus.

PRESTON ATKINSON, Senior Pastor, Sunbury Bible Church

Kerry puts words and testimony to the beliefs we hold on to but don't know how to access. *Stand* gives us a road map out of despair and into tremendous hope.

DR. ERICA MCELROY, ER Physician, Founder, Hava Foundation and Casa Materna Atitlán

The Way of Becoming is practical and profoundly spiritual. It is Kerry's stewardship of God's lavish and intricate beauty. She desires to obey and teach what and when God asks and points all to Jesus.

JONI YOUNG, Biblical Lay Counselor

STAND

Kerry Hasenbalg

2 Cor. 3:18

KERRY HASENBALG

Cover art and design: Mark Ford, Samantha Frolich, and Georgine Patt
Interior design: Brandi Davis
Author photo credit: Annika Hasenbalg

First printing edition: 2025

Blue House Books
PO Box 205
Riverside, PA 17868

Printed in the United States of America

info@thebecomingacademy.com
www.kerryhasenbalg.com

I dedicate this work of *Stand* to Jesus, my anchor,
and to Scott, my "cross-tie" in every storm.

CONTENTS

Stand is being released in recognition of the 70th year
of the eternal life of Billy Marks, the 17th year of the
eternal life of Isabella Grace Hasenbalg, and in partnership
with the 2025 National Day of Prayer.

I praise God for fulfilling His promise to give beauty for ashes.

FOREWORD

God often places treasures in our path throughout our journey, and for me, meeting Kerry Hasenbalg was like finding an entire treasure chest overflowing with God's glorious riches. From the moment we connected through our mutual friend, artist Julie Ann Scott, it was clear that God had orchestrated our paths to cross for His purposes. Through prayer and partnership, this booklet, *Stand*, comes to you—a powerful resource born of faith, resilience, and a commitment to stand firm in the storms of life.

When Kerry offered me the privilege of writing the foreword for STAND, one of the twelve practices she teaches in her book *The Way of Becoming*, I wanted to run and grab my laptop and start typing. I assumed I would pull from what God had already imparted to me regarding our call to stand . . . but I was wrong. God would call me to stand and wait. Like a scribe, I waited, ready with my pen, watching and listening for specific words from the Spirit, a whisper, that still, small voice (1 Kings 19:12).

But instead of a still, small voice, I received a storm . . . two storms, actually: one named Helene and another named Milton. Having a home in Florida and many friends and family there, we watched and prayed as each storm formed, strengthened, approached, and made landfall. While meteorologists attempt to describe the power of the wind, waves, and rain, nothing exhibits a storm's force more clearly than when they go out and stand in it. Like meteorologists braving hurricanes to provide crucial insights, God calls us to stand firm in prayer during the storms we encounter.

Stand is more than a booklet; it is a guide to spiritual resilience, offering encouragement and practical wisdom to equip us for life's trials. It is an invitation to step into God's calling with courage and conviction. Paired with the 2025 National Day of Prayer's theme song, "I Will Stand" (co-written by Kerry), this work serves as a rallying cry for all of us to stand in the truth of God's love and embrace our role as intercessors, standing in the gap for those in need.

In these pages, Kerry not only shares her deeply personal testimony of one of the most significant storms of her life, but she also provides a survivor's guide on how we can stand in suffering and the battle plan for standing in victory. As you read Kerry's tender account and reflect on the truth she shares, may you be inspired to stand firm amid your own trials and on behalf of others, proclaiming God's eternal goodness. Together, let us glorify Him through every storm, trusting in His promise to strengthen and sustain us. Prepare to armor up, pray up, and STAND!

Serving Him with Gladness,

KATHY BRANZELL
President, National Day of Prayer Task Force

INTRODUCTION

There are moments in the life of every human story when we must gather up everything we have known, learned, and believed and anchor ourselves in the deep as the storm approaches.

The text you are about to read, STAND, is only an excerpt of a much larger work. It is *one* of the twelve practices the Lord revealed to me as I "considered the ancient paths" revealed in the words of Scripture and in God's creation and asked Him how to apply each of these practices to my life. Thus, the work of STAND represents a piece of a greater story playing out in each of our lives as God reveals Himself to us personally and collectively. Over the last two decades, I have shared these teachings and these tools with thousands of people, how these practices have borne fruit in my life despite many losses and trials, and how every believer can experience similar fruit in their own lives.

The purpose of sharing my story is not so you will become an observer of my life, but so you will become an explorer in your own. At the end of this booklet, you will find a section called Your Becoming Story, encouraging you to search for parallel truths in your own experiences and consider their connections to God's promises. While this chapter can exist independently, I highly recommend receiving this text as an appetizer before enjoying the soul-nourishing feast that the twelve practices offer in my book *The Way of Becoming*.

The Way of Becoming is a collection of stories bathed in Scripture and written as an invitation and a guide to lead you further along the ancient paths of the Christian faith. Its twelve faith practices show you how to experience a deeper, more intimate relationship with God and recognize His empowering presence in your story. Together, they reveal The *How* of Faith in the *Now* of Life and equip us for the days in which we live.

Meanwhile, my friend, know this: You have been put on earth for such a time as this. It is by no accident that you are reading this text, and I pray you sense the beckoning of your Maker: "*Take courage, Stand up! He is calling for you*" (Mark 10:49 NASB).

STAND

In Paul's letter to the Ephesians, he calls on believers to clothe themselves in the armor of God so that "when the day of evil comes, you may be able to stand your ground" (Ephesians 6:13). The words "day of evil" always seemed a little excessive to me . . . until one day, the gates of hell themselves came against my family, and every one of my beliefs was tested.

My brother's wife, Jenn, and I were both pregnant at the same time. It was the first week of January 2008, one week before Jenn's due date and three weeks before mine, when my husband Scott's brother-in-law, Jim, had a heart attack. Scott packed his suitcase and flew out to South Carolina the next day to be with his sister and help care for their baby so she could be with her husband in the hospital. Meanwhile, my parents came to help me care for our two young children while Scott was away since I was so far along in my pregnancy. Soon after Scott left and my parents arrived, my sister-in-law Jenn went into labor.

My parents, my two kids, and I immediately left our house in the Poconos, which was about an hour from the hospital. We wanted to make it back to our hometown when my brother Bobby and Jenn's baby would be born. On the way home, our son Cole became violently ill and started vomiting in the car. Just then, Bobby called my father. Dad picked up and said, "Bob, I can't talk; Cole just threw up everywhere. Call you back." In the chaos of the moment, Dad didn't hear his son's reply. Bobby had yelled out on the other end of the phone, "Wait, Dad!"

When Dad called him back, Bobby was sitting alone in a hospital room, not knowing if he would ever see his wife or infant son alive again. Jenn's epidural had gone to her heart, and both mom and baby had flatlined. They'd been rushed out of the delivery room, and Bobby still had no word on their condition. When we finally arrived at the hospital, we found Bobby holding his newborn son alive while still waiting to hear whether his wife would survive. Ultimately, through a series of long-shot medical interventions intermingled with a series of divine interventions, both son and mother were miraculously saved.

WHEN DARKNESS FALLS

As I lay down in bed later that night, it occurred to me that I had not felt my baby move all day. I figured I was just distracted by the day's trying events. Scott flew back home late that night. Exhausted, I fell asleep praying for God's help and protection. The following day was January 6, Scott's birthday and the holy day of Epiphany, which was both strange and fitting considering the integration of human storylines that would continue to play out.

My mom offered to watch our kids so Scott and I could catch up and have a private birthday brunch for him. When we sat down, I shared my worries with him about not noticing any baby movement. Scott took me straight to the hospital, where we were taken to the labor and delivery floor. Through an ultrasound, we were informed that what we had feared most had actually come to pass: our baby no longer had a heartbeat.

It's difficult to describe the pain that overswept me in an instant. I began to cry out in utterly despairing grief—at a level that was beyond my understanding. It was as if I were witnessing myself wailing from outside of my body. My brother, Bobby, could hear my cries from their hospital room just across the hall. He did not know it was his sister crying, but he began to pray, knowing that this sound must be a mother who had just lost her child; the cry he heard was unlike any other.

I had only ever heard this "otherworldly" sound of distress when I witnessed a Ugandan woman fall apart at the news that her baby had been stolen. While in Africa, I learned that this weeping and screaming combination was known as keening. The people there had grown quite familiar with its sound, as terrorists had abducted tens of thousands of children in that region in recent years.[1] I, too, felt my child had been stolen.

Two Doors Apart

I was placed in a wheelchair and taken down the hall to where a second ultrasound would confirm our baby's death. Scott walked beside me, and we both began quietly worshiping just to keep breathing. Three years earlier, the miscarriage of our daughter Malaya had taught us the importance of singing praise just to regain our breath when the pain is all-consuming. This type of worship was not some kind of celebration in the high notes of life but a choice to cling to God as our Breath-Giver in the low notes of life for our survival.

---

1. "Abducted: The Lord's Resistance Army and Forced Conscription in Northern Uganda," Harvard Humanitarian Initiative, n.d., https://hhi.harvard.edu/ publications/abducted-lords-resistance-army-and-forced-conscription-northern.

When the second ultrasound confirmed our child's passing, we also found out for the first time that our baby was a girl. The nurses took us to a room only two doors down from my older brother, where his wife and baby were recovering. The contrast could not have been more stark: I could not have imagined that our family would experience "the House of Rejoicing" and "the House of Mourning" two doors apart in the same hospital.

Only God could be what we each needed now.

Doctors informed me that labor must be promptly induced. After the life-threatening complication that had almost taken my sister-in-law's life, I decided to forgo having an epidural. As I climbed into the hospital bed to begin the laboring process, Scott said, "I'm sorry, Honey . . . I can't help you now."

"I know you can't," I replied straightaway. This was another understanding I had gained earlier, albeit in lesser trials. If this had happened in our first years of marriage, I would have had greater expectations of Scott to be some kind of savior rather than my companion in the suffering. It is natural to look to our spouse to fix what ails us. But I knew only God could be what each of us needed now.

Our baby girl was in a place only He was familiar with.

I slid my body to one side of the bed and invited Scott to lie beside me while I labored to release the shell that no longer housed our baby's spirit. The pain that accompanied my labor, without the epidural, was a strange comfort to me, as it provided a physical embodiment of the profound grief I was feeling over the loss of my child.

During one of the relief points in the laboring process, we talked about what we should name our daughter. Though we would not be raising her, we had already learned the importance of naming the children carried in my womb. We wanted to find a name that would minister to our broken hearts when we spoke of her. The Spirit led us to the sixty-first chapter of Isaiah, which discusses Christ's ministry to those who suffer. We chose the name *Isabella Grace,* or *Bella* for short, based on God's promise to give "beauty for ashes" (KJV). Her full name affirmed God's promise to give us beauty for ashes. Bella meant *beautiful,* Isabella, *consecrated*, and Grace, the *empowering presence of God.* By faith, we trusted that our daughter was now consecrated in the empowering presence of God and that her legacy would be one of beauty in exchange for the ashes we would entrust to our Lord at her burial.

Later in this long laboring process, I asked Scott, now sitting in the chair beside the bed and reading his Bible,

"What are you reading?"

"Ecclesiastes 7:3," he answered. "'Sorrow is better than laughter because sorrow has a refining influence on us'" (NLT).

I can't quite understand that right now, I thought. But I held on to the words, hoping they might make sense later.

Silently, my mind turned inward, and I entered into the practice that had become familiar over many years . . . to bring my wrestling to God and to ask Him my questions directly.

First, I wondered if this was happening because God loved me less than others. So, I asked Him. And His Holy Spirit answered by reminding me of children I had known and come to love through my orphan care ministry, who had also suffered deeply. The Spirit asked me to consider His love for a girl I knew named Jeanne.

BETWEEN THE ASKED AND ANSWERED

Jeanne had suffered unimaginable horrors most of us could not even imagine. As a nine-year-old, she had witnessed her parents' brutal death during the Rwandan genocide against the Tutsis in 1994. She was later brought to the United States by a Rwandan foster family. In truth, she had been separated from her many siblings—including her own twin sister—to experience labor exploitation and to be abused by the family's father. When I met Jeanne, the Lord filled me with inexplicable love for her, and over many years, she and her siblings, who still lived in Africa, became like family to me. I had witnessed firsthand how profoundly God loved them and how He could—and *did*—redeem their suffering for the salvation of many.[2] Their stories taught me that God had been with them through their hardships and that His love was more immense than even the most profound human suffering.

So, when I asked if God loved me less and He answered me by reminding me of Jeanne, it revealed that He had not stopped loving me any more than He had stopped loving her.

Soon, another question surfaced: *Lord, did You take my baby because of* my *sin? Is this how it works even after repentance and salvation?* I wondered, so I asked Him. God reminded me of His servant Job and how he, who was called the most righteous man on the earth during his lifetime, had lost all ten of his children in a single moment when the day of evil came upon him. Even then, Job did not sin against God. Instead, he recognized the Lord's sovereignty in his ultimate sorrow, saying, "Naked I came from my mother's womb, and naked I will depart.

---

2. Celestine Lakin, *A Voice in the Darkness: Memoir of a Rwandan Genocide Survivor* (Wheeler & James, 2018).

The LORD gave and the LORD has taken away; may the name of the LORD be praised" (Job 1:21). The Scriptures reveal that Job's soul remained intact through his tribulation period because he was determined not to speak against God and maintain his integrity (Job 27:5). Integrity is about holding firmly to the things we have already come to believe so that we can remain standing despite the hurricanes in our midst, and even while we wrestle to overcome our unbelief. Remembering Job's innocence juxtaposed with his profound suffering comforted me and helped me continue to STAND in faith.

Still, I wondered: *When all this has passed, will I be so damaged on the other side that I won't even recognize myself?*

In reply, a vision came to my mind's eye. Glancing over to the labor and delivery room corner, I saw a blazing fire with people standing inside it. I knew the story of Shadrach, Meshach, and Abednego and how they had been thrown into Nebuchadnezzar's fiery furnace, so I assumed it was them I was seeing. But as I looked closer, I realized it wasn't them. Instead, I saw Scott, Jesus, and me standing together in those flames. The vision brought me deep comfort and caused a small new flame of hope to stir deep in my soul. But the pain of our loss, as my body labored in delivery, still hung over me like thick darkness.

"Later you will understand"

In this cloudy haze, I asked Scott, "Honey, what are you thinking about?"

He replied, "I can't seem to get the lyrics of one of Steve's songs out of my head. I keep hearing, 'You are being loved right now. There's a song being sung over you by the One who breathed life into you. You are being loved right now at this very moment.'"[3] Scott paused. Then, he spoke again. "It sounds strange, I know, but it keeps replaying in my mind."

How could this be love? How could God be singing over us right now in our devasting loss? I couldn't imagine.

> **We have this hope as an anchor for the soul.**

Still, I chose to hold on to this idea because of what Jesus had told His disciples. "You do not realize now what I am doing, but later you will understand" (John 13:7). I understood some things at that point in my journey, and other things I still did not. The fact that God loved me all the time was something I believed theoretically, but at that moment, I didn't feel very loved. Still, God reminded me of how I had

3. Steven Curtis Chapman. "You are Being Loved." *This Moment.* Sparrow Records. 2007, Spotify.

felt His love flow through me for others who were suffering and didn't feel loved. Numb and overwhelmed as I was, I knew my God had answered me before, so I chose to wait for Him to bring understanding again.

The day we left the hospital, we received an email from Steven Curtis Chapman, with whom Scott was working in ministry. Steve was on a writers' retreat in Ireland with several other worship leaders when he heard about the loss of our baby. He asked the other retreat participants to pray with him. That night, God impressed the verses Hebrews 6:19–20 on the heart of another worship leader, Matt Redman, concerning our loss. "We have this hope as an anchor for the soul, firm and secure. It enters the inner sanctuary behind the curtain, where our forerunner, Jesus, has entered on our behalf."

Matt and Steve began to pen a song based on that verse the following day. Then Steven and his son Caleb stayed up late into the night recording the song so we would have it as a source of comfort as soon as we returned home from the hospital without our baby girl.

And so, it turned out that Scott had spoken prophetically when he felt the reality that the Maker of heaven and earth was singing over us. The truth of Scott's words emanated through the song written and recorded called

"Close to Your Heart," based on Hebrews 6:19, where hope in Jesus Christ is referred to as "an anchor for the soul."[4] I was grateful for the comfort this song brought me in the early days after our loss. I would repeat lines from the lyrics frequently as a way of soothing my soul and when trying to fall asleep in the hard weeks that followed.

ANCHORED AND CROSS-TIED

The more I listened, the more another question began niggling within me: *What good is an anchor in a hurricane?*

Indeed, what we were experiencing was no ordinary storm; it was a hurricane. This was the day that evil had come against my entire family, threatening three of its members and taking the life of our baby girl, Isabella Grace. At delivery, we learned that there was a knot in her cord, which had suddenly tightened and cut off her supply of oxygen.

The grief felt like it would consume me; it felt as though I was drawing closer and closer to the eyewall of the storm. I wondered if the brokenness was permanent and whether I would return to wholeness.

---

4. Steven Curtis Chapman. "Close to Your Heart (feat. Matt Redman)." *Safe in the Arms.* Sparrow Records. 2010, Spotify.

So, I continued to take my grievances to God in the form of questions. Dialoguing with Him was already part of our way together. My thoughts and questions went something like this: *You created language, every word, every created thing, water itself, even the molecules that comprise water, and the atoms that make up all things. You created boats and even the idea of boats, anchors, and people making boats and being in boats. So, if You called our hope an anchor, allowed this hurricane to hit us, and inspired these men to write this song, then please help me understand what this means for me now. What good is an anchor when trying to survive a hurricane?*

Boats and Docks

I searched for God's truth regarding anchors and storms in science and language. The document I discovered was a transcript from a lecture given to boat owners at the National Marine Hurricane Preparation Symposium on how a boat can survive a hurricane. Even though it was not a spiritual message, it read like a parable to me.

The lecturer, David Pascoe, began by saying,

The dock anchoring brochure was picked up twice as often as the information on direct anchorage. But this will change over the course of the year when the marinas discover that a boat on an anchor mooring is ten times more likely to survive than a boat tied to a dock. As a matter of fact, the dock has a much better chance of surviving if boats are not tied to it during a hurricane. Almost all docks will survive a hurricane when no boats are tied to them.[5]

The message was expressed in maritime jargon. But as I read the document, the Holy Spirit seemed to play the role of simultaneous translator, causing me to comprehend the deeper spiritual meanings of the illustrations mentioned. "Boats" were human souls. "Docks" represent things we can see with our eyes in this world. Tying our hopes to something we can see is like hitching a boat to a dock in a storm. Placing our hopes in the truth of Christ and God's Word is the same as dropping anchor into the depths of the sea by "direct anchorage."

Anything we tether to apart from the Lord only gives us a false sense of safety.

Whenever we see a storm coming, we must consider the strength of what we have tied our hopes to for survival. Suppose it is something we can see with our eyes, as docks can be seen, like our homes,

5. Pascoe, "Safe Harbor—How to Protect Your Boats From Storms," National Marine Hurricane Preparation Symposium, 2008.

jobs, ministries, wealth, health, stuff, looks, past successes, or reputations. In these cases, we must know that these things will not keep us safe through life's great tribulations, such as the death of a child, divorce, betrayal, disease, abuse, war, disaster, or facing our own mortality.

God calls us to evaluate what we have become wrongly tied to as a source of hope or security. Whatever it may be—anything we tether to other than the Lord—only gives us a false sense of safety that will fall apart when the storm comes, putting *both* us and what we are tied to in jeopardy. The untethering process requires self-examination and the cutting loose of harmful soul-ties that would tear us apart in a hurricane. In times of crisis involving life and death, when it is beyond the ability of things and people to save, the only thing that will keep our boats in one piece is to anchor directly into the unseen presence of God.

I began to see that this way of anchoring is precisely what it means to STAND when the day of evil comes.

As I read further, I learned ways to minimize loss and damage in a storm, which I found particularly relevant to our relationships with other "boats," that is, people.

It read, "The domino effect occurs when one boat on a canal breaks loose and crashes into others, resulting in a chain reaction that ends up with boats piled up at the end of the canal."[6] Pascoe used the example of the aftermath of Hurricane Andrew, where hundreds upon hundreds of boats were piled up at the end of the canals due to this domino effect.

The lecturer warned, "Therefore, consider whether your boat will be vulnerable to the domino effect when contemplating whether to cross-tie to another boat. If possible, try to check on the anchorage of the boats upwind from you. If someone's done a lousy job or has been tied to weak or rotten docks, then, chances are, his boat is going to wreck yours."[7]

Where Hope Is Anchored

When Scott told me, "I can't help you," I already knew I could not anchor my hopes in Scott. He could not answer my soul's most pressing questions nor care for our daughter, who was now gone from this earth, and he could not heal my broken heart. We each needed to anchor directly into Jesus ourselves. And so we did. We could lie side by side and cross-tie to one another for support and comfort, sharing things God was ministering to us individually. But we would need our own sustenance and rescue by being anchored in the Lord for our souls' wholeness and integrity.

6. Pascoe, "Safe Harbor."
7. Pascoe, "Safe Harbor."

This maritime expert also wrote, "You'll probably stand a better chance if you can use anchors to stand off from the dock, or find a better location, rather than being a sitting duck at the end of the canal." Pascoe emphasized this: "If you don't know how well they have anchored, it's better to stand off alone, but be aware that you will face an inevitable disaster if the storm comes and you are tied to a boat with no anchor."[8]

Because boats represent people, these maritime realities about anchoring in a storm confirm that it is better to be alone, away from the crowd, than around many other people who have not chosen to place their hopes in Christ when a storm is coming.

Though being anchored alone is better than being with others who have failed to anchor themselves in the deep, the best thing is what maritime experts call the *neighborhood team effect*:

> If you can generate a neighborhood team effect, so much the better. But you have to get all the boat owners involved and ensure that all the boats are well secured by their own anchors. Many boats survived the eye of Hurricane Andrew despite fronting directly

8. Pascoe, "Safe Harbor."

on Biscayne Bay, with a 10-foot storm surge, by a combination of cross-tying and anchors.[9]

According to maritime experts and God's Word, the best way to survive a hurricane and remain standing is through a combination of anchoring in Christ and cross-tying to those who are also anchored in Him. If we want our boat, that is, our soul, to survive with its integrity still intact on the other side of a great storm, we must choose to anchor into Jesus and cross-tie with others who have also anchored in the depths of the Lord themselves.

FELLOWSHIP OF THE SUFFERING

God not only provided these profound truths that would minister to my soul in this season of tribulation but also the vessels of His grace in the form of others who had suffered with whom I could cross-tie. From early on in my pregnancy, when I asked the Lord for a name for our child that reflected our season of life, He only gave me the name Jacob. So, for a time, I thought we were having a boy. But a few months before my due date, my sister-in-law Jenn announced they were having a boy and naming him Jacob. *Hmm,* I thought. *Maybe God is just speaking to me about my*

9. Pascoe, "Safe Harbor."

nephew. But as it turns out, God had more to share with me about the name Jacob in light of my story.

Even though my Rwandan friend, Jeanne, had not yet heard we had lost our baby, she emailed me telling me how the Lord had put me on her heart and called her to pray for me. She quoted directly from the book of Isaiah, referencing me as a type of Jacob and saying God had given her this verse for me:

> But now, this is what the Lord says—he who created you, Jacob, he who formed you, Israel: "Do not fear, for I have redeemed you; I have summoned you by name; you are mine. When you pass through the waters, I will be with you; and when you pass through the rivers, they will not sweep over you. When you walk through the fire, you will not be burned; the flames will not set you ablaze. For I am the Lord your God, the Holy One of Israel, your Savior." (Isaiah 43:1–3)

When God spoke the name Jacob to me, He was speaking prophetically so that, in time, I would understand more about my soul's wrestling. Jacob's wrestling with God was about his journey of relenting before God's power and *becoming* changed in the process.

Just as God was with Jacob, He was faithful to see me through the raging fires and the violent waters. I was not burned up, drowned, or destroyed. Instead, God sang over Scott and me in the storm. He answered all my desperate cries and questions. He reminded me again and again of His presence and His love. Yes, death comes to us all and all our loved ones. But only those who press in to ask, seek, and knock will receive the answers, healing, and provisions they seek. Sorrows and sufferings are like seeds planted in our souls. If these seeds are watered with God's Word and given the light of His wisdom, they will, in time, grow up and produce fruit that can be shared for the comfort and nourishment of others.

A Life Raft

The weeks following our daughter's death were extremely tough, with waves of grief befalling without notice. I usually felt the Lord's comforting presence draw close during these times. But when I would cross out of mourning and into self-pity, thinking no one else could understand my pain, the comfort I needed would often seem far off. I cried to the Lord, who showed me how to find His comfort again. He took me to 1 Peter 5:9, which says, "Resist him [the enemy], standing firm in the faith, because you know that the family of believers throughout the world is undergoing the same kinds of sufferings." I sensed the Lord was encouraging me to remember that I am not alone in my suffering and that there was wisdom and support to be gleaned from those in His body who had gone before me.

I remember sitting at my dining room table when my breast milk came in and thinking, *I should be nursing my baby, not planning her funeral.* In this time of grief, my father's brother Vic called to offer the other half of their baby brother's grave for Isabella to be buried. My grandmother, Mema, who had been a spiritual mentor to me, had lost her youngest child, Billy, at the age of two in a drowning accident. My uncle Vic had witnessed it but could not save his brother because he was only three years old himself at the time and could not swim yet either. Other people cannot save us from experiencing pain and suffering, but they can make the road we walk a little easier and the loads we carry a little lighter if we let them.

My Isabella and Mema's Billy would share a grave plot because both were small, having died so young. In time, I realized that God meant the sharing of this burial plot as far more than a way of lightening my hardship. It was an image of the spiritual understanding that Mema had entrusted to me over the years, which had come out of her wrestling with God, combined with the spiritual insights that came out of mine. The Lord showed me that

STAND

I was experiencing a unique kind of fellowship of mothers who have suffered the loss of their children. Mema and I joined this fellowship outside of time. Through its initiation, I began applying the many lessons she had taught me out of her seeking and finding God in the darkness. In a way, Mema had handed me a life raft before I knew I would need it. Only the Lord knew that she would be with Him when her life lessons would need to be applied to mine. I sensed that somehow and someday, the mixed ashes of our children will become part of the beauty that will adorn the head of Christ's resurrected bride.

STRESS WOOD

Knowing that storms come on us suddenly, it is critical to gather provisions and develop healthy relationships in advance so that when the storms come, we can remain standing. The analogy of anchoring in Christ and cross-tying to other believers can also be found in creation, inviting us all to apply the concepts to our lives. A tree's anchor is its taproot, which is first sent straight down deep into the soil to secure the tree before it can rise. Next, it sends out its branching roots that eventually intertwine, or cross-tie, with the branches of other trees underground.

Branching roots can be pervasive. Take, for instance, the branching roots of a single well-developed oak tree, which can even go out for over a hundred miles if laid from end to end. But no matter how impressive a tree's branching roots may be, just like some people's extensive social networks may seem impressive, neither a tree's branching roots nor a person's social networks will be sufficient to save them if the storm blows too strong. It may actually be their downfall; as one goes, so go the others, falling like dominoes if they lack proper taproots. Remember, the taproot is the tree's main anchor. The more trees in an area with deep taproots and healthy branching roots that are intertwined with other deeply rooted trees, the less likely it is that the forest will become decimated in a hurricane.

Rooted and Grounded

God desires His children to live in healthy spiritual communities so they can experience His character and love through the people with whom their lives are intertwined. When the apostle Paul speaks of a healthy community, using the terms "rooted" and "grounded" in Christ, it should evoke the image of the underground root systems in a thriving forest. Paul prayed,

> that He would grant you, according to the riches of
> His glory, to be strengthened with power through

His Spirit in the inner self, so that Christ may
dwell in your hearts through faith; and that you,
being rooted and grounded in love, may be able to
comprehend with all the saints what is the width
and length and height and depth, and to know
the love of Christ which surpasses knowledge,
that you may be filled to all the fullness of God.
(Ephesians 3:16–19 NASB)

For trees to become deeply rooted and grounded, wind
is essential. Without the wind, trees grow weak, thin, and
underdeveloped in their root systems. When exposed to
strong winds, trees form something called stress wood,
which is necessary for their survival. Stress wood, also called
tension wood or reaction wood, enables trees to grow toward
the light for optimal sun exposure and to remain standing
strong in a storm. Stress wood vastly improves a tree's ability
to withstand hurricane-force winds. Even though trees can
grow much more quickly when shielded from the wind,
they will not develop stress wood and, therefore, will not be
able to sustain the weight accompanying their height. This
was proven in a scientific experiment called Biosphere 2,
where the trees were shielded entirely from wind and, as
a result, did not develop the core strength they needed to

reach maturity and sustain themselves.[10]

So it is with us. The small trials we face daily test the composition of our faith and reveal whether or not the hope we are holding on to is secure and able to withstand when the winds of life pick up. Standing is meant to be something we do every day in small ways. Daily anchoring into the presence of God amidst the "ordinary" trials of daily life, like annoyances in relationships, aging, or minor illnesses, gives us a chance to grow stronger and become more deeply rooted. Seeking to remove every force that comes against us is like asking God to stop the wind from blowing through the trees.

Even before this experience of such painful, personal loss, I struggled with the Bible verses in Romans 5:3–5 that call us to rejoice in our sufferings. Paul says, "We also glory in our sufferings, because we know that suffering produces perseverance; perseverance, character; and character, hope. And hope does not put us to shame." I could see how suffering can lead to perseverance and even to character development, but hope? It just did not compute. At least, not until my desperation for a new kind of eternal hope forced my own taproot to drop deeper into the things of

10. Aidan McCullen, "Organisational Stress Wood: Struggle Builds Resilience," *The Innovation Show*, June 30, 2022. https://theinnovationshow.io/organisational-stress-wood-struggle-builds-resilience/.

God and, in time, caused my mind to rise higher toward the things of heaven. Once again, I returned to the parable of the trees. They must send their taproots deep before their trunks can be raised to the heights and remain standing.

Standing is something we practice both in the storms and extended times of waiting. *Stand* means occupying a place, being on one's feet, or "being ready." Standing is not about using our energy or will to move forward, but rather, getting up, staying up, and getting back up so we don't lose ground in life's buffeting or times of waiting. Romans 12:12 describes the proper posture for spiritual standing: "Be joyful in hope, patient in affliction, faithful in prayer." Two closely related words can help us better engage in this faith practice of standing—withstand and understand.

To *withstand* means to have the power and ability to remain standing when things come against us and test our resolve. The ability to withstand is based on what something or someone has already become, what they consist of, and what provisions they have been able to gather before facing the storms, battles, or times of waiting. Essentially, what are we standing *with*? The more reconciled and integrated our souls become, the better we can withstand what tests us.

Understanding means standing in the midst of, beneath, or within, and it is something we gain by receiving, putting together, or grasping. Therefore, the biblical call to gain understanding is about doing the vital work of investigating truth and putting our thoughts and experiences together with the truth of God's Word. This faith work we do before coming into a trial curates the provision, protection, and confidence in Christ we need to get through it.

On Guard and Alert

We are called to remain alert and on guard, trusting even when God seems silent, absent, or when our hopes have been deferred. To encourage my faith in the times of waiting, I hung a giant wooden sign in my home with a quote found etched on the wall of a German concentration camp during WWII. It reads, "I believe in the sun even when it is not shining. I believe in love even when I cannot feel it. I believe in God even when He is silent."

Knowing what we have already become in Him according to our understanding of His love and truth can give us the confidence and courage to STAND in trials or times of waiting. Our understanding of the Word and our confident beliefs in Christ are like spiritual armor that covers and protects us.

Put on the full armor of God, so that when the day of evil comes, you may be able to stand your ground, and after you have done everything, continue to stand. Stand firm then, with the belt of truth buckled around your waist, with the breastplate of righteousness in place, and with your feet fitted with the readiness that comes from the gospel of peace. In addition to all this, take up the shield of faith, with which you can extinguish all the flaming arrows of the evil one. Take the helmet of salvation and the sword of the Spirit, which is the Word of God. And pray in the Spirit on all occasions with all kinds of prayers and requests. With this in mind, be alert, and always keep praying for all the Lord's people. (Ephesians 6:13–18)

These verses teach us that by being clothed in God's righteousness, peace, truth, and the memories of His savings, as well as being equipped with tools of faith and the Word of God, we will be able to STAND our ground when the strong winds buffet and turmoil encompasses us like a hurricane. God's grace in these forms will be sufficient for us to remain standing; it calls on the "spiritual stress wood" that has been developed in our souls. Four pieces of spiritual clothing need to be intentionally "put on": the belt of truth, the breastplate of righteousness, the helmet of salvation, and the shoes of peace. Not only are we called to "put on" certain things, but we are also called to "take up" spiritual tools, which involve deliberate actions of faith. They are the shield of faith, the sword of the Spirit, and words of prayer.

The sword of the Spirit, which is the Word of God, is the only offensive weapon mentioned, and it is the power by which you can push back the darkness. By taking up our armor, anchoring in the living presence of God, and cross-tying with other believers who are likewise anchored and "standing," we can defend ourselves against evil.

> The call to every believer is to be faithful in every possible way we can and to STAND on the Lord's promises.

Indeed, once we are clothed and armed, God tells us three times that we are simply called to STAND, "so that when the day of evil comes, you may be able to stand your ground, and after you have done everything, to stand. Stand firm then" (Ephesians 6:13–14a). He is the One who will do the fighting for us. Our job is to keep watch, remain steadfast, and continue in prayer. "You will not have to fight this battle. Take up your positions; stand firm and see the deliverance the LORD will give you, Judah and Jerusalem. Do not be afraid; do not be discouraged. Go out to face them tomorrow, and the LORD will be with you" (2 Chronicles 20:17). The call to every believer is to be faithful in every possible way we can and to STAND on the promise that it is the Lord who fights our battles and will bring about our rescue.

Going into battle with God makes me think of how a father often dances with his young daughter. Though both may be twirling around the floor, he is doing all the work while she stands on his feet, merely along for the ride. The same principle was at work when the Israelites overcame hardship and won their battles and when God told David to pick up five smooth stones. And with one stone and slingshot, David felled the giant (1 Samuel 17:49–50). God allowed Joshua to bring down the walls of Jericho by simply walking, praising, and blowing a ram's horn (Joshua 6:20). Moses only had to touch the waters of the Red Sea for God to part them (Exodus 14:21). And he needed only to strike the rock as God said so that water would flow from it (Exodus 17:6). The power to overcome was not in the stone, sling, horn, or staff. His power is in the grace He provides to those willing to take tiny, obedient steps of faith: anchoring in the deep, picking up our battle gear, remaining clothed in His righteousness, surrendering to His providence amidst the hurricane, and then doing all we can to STAND while the Lord delivers the victory.

"I WILL STAND"

In the dark
Do You hear me?
In the loss
Do You see me?
In the night
Time moves slowly.
In the wait, will You hold me?

In hopes and fears
In unmet dreams
In troubled days
That You'll redeem

I will stand on Your truth,
My heart stands.
In Your Word, I place my hope.
My soul waits for You, Lord,
My soul waits.
In between the asked and answered,
Even when I'm bruised and battered,
I will stand and wait and trust in You, Lord.

In the light
I can see You.

STAND

In the warmth,
I can feel You.
In the day,
Hope comes quickly.
In the wait,
You have held me.

I guard my soul.
I keep the walls.
I will not doubt,
When darkness falls

I've done all that I can do.
Now, I'll watch and wait for You.
Like the sunrise in the East,
Rays of love will bring me peace.

In the wait, I've grown stronger.
I will fear the dark no longer.
I will watch for Your coming,
More than those who wait for morning.[11]

---

11. Kerry Hasenbalg, "I Will Stand," featuring Melodee DeVevo, Becoming Collective, 2024, Spotify.

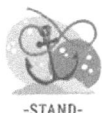

-STAND-

YOUR *BECOMING* STORY: STAND

Each of us must be equipped for the storms that life brings us. Whether the "slow erode" or the "sudden shattering" of a hurricane—suffering is ubiquitous. Everyone experiences some measure of "the day of evil," and thus Paul's command rings out to each of us: *"And after you have done everything . . . stand"* (Ephesians 6:13).

It behooves us to examine ourselves and ask: *Am I ready for a hurricane?*

Do I know how to STAND?

Four keys are necessary for a believer to prepare to STAND in the day of evil.

First, consider your "boat," or soul. It must be cleaned and ready for action. Walking in forgiveness for those who have wronged you, entrusting your hurts to the Lord for healing, and confessing your sins regularly are critical to accessing intimacy with God and experiencing the blessings of His empowering presence. Be relentless in "dialogue with God" in both the high and low notes of everyday life.

Second, assess your anchorage. *What are you anchored to?* This requires unfettered honesty and openness, allowing the Holy Spirit to search your heart. What do you cling to for comfort and security? Success? Relationships? Finances? Reputation? Stuff? Your soul's anchor must be dropped into the depth of God's love and faithful presence. Take the time to cut the soul-ties that will harm you in a storm. Cast off the idols and distractions so that nothing takes the place of God as the Savior of your life.

Third, assess your "cross-ties." Are you living in a healthy, faith-filled community, able to experience the "neighborhood team effect"? God has provided His body as a means for loving and strengthening you, including during the worst storms one can endure. Consider the fellowship that can be found with those who have gone before you in their own journeys of suffering and come out the other side with wisdom to share. If you are not in honest, consistent, and healthy relationships with other believers anchored to God's presence, consider asking the Lord to connect you in new ways to His living body and help you invest in relationships that will bear eternal fruit.

Fourth, embrace the winds of daily life. Build your "stress wood" and prepare for the larger storms. How have you seen God amid your suffering? How has your suffering produced godly character in you or given you more of an eternal perspective? Ask yourself what your faith consists of. What are you made of? Consider the integrated beliefs you have on board your soul that have served as provision and protection during times of trial. What Scriptures can you attach to these experiences; what of God's Word has been proven true in your life?

> God is our refuge and strength,
>   an ever-present help in trouble.
> Therefore we will not fear, though the earth give way
>   and the mountains fall into the heart of the sea,
> though its waters roar and foam
>   and the mountains quake with their surging.
>
> There is a river whose streams make glad the
>   city of God,
>   the holy place where the Most High dwells.
> God is within her, she will not fall;
>   God will help her at break of day.
> Nations are in uproar, kingdoms fall;
>   he lifts his voice, the earth melts.
>
> The Lord Almighty is with us;
>   the God of Jacob is our fortress. (Psalm 46:1–7)

If *Stand* gave you hope and a desire to explore more of your own *becoming* story in God, then we invite you to continue on your journey toward wholeness. *Stand* represents only one of the twelve practices highlighted in Kerry's guide for soul care, *The Way of Becoming.*

By using the tools from *The Way of Becoming,* God's Word will come alive in your story. You will learn how to apply each faith practice to your trying circumstances, the complexities of your relationships, and your soul's condition. Journey with Kerry on her faith-filled adventures around the globe, from an untouchable village in India to the presidential palace of China, from the African savannah to an underground Metro in Russia. Empower your soul to rise out of the places where it has been transfixed by fear and become transformed by grace.

Come discover the "*how* of faith in the *now* of life."

The Twelve Practices from *The Way of Becoming*

1. Believe	**7. Stand**
2. Remember	8. Praise
3. Ask	9. Anoint
4. Imagine	10. Create
5. Trust	11. Assemble
6. Redeem	12. Abide

www.kerryhasenbalg.com

ACKNOWLEDGMENTS

I want to thank Kathy Branzell and the National Day of Prayer Task Force for their partnership, support of my work, and their ongoing dedication to calling the people of our nation to prayer. I am humbled to have this work of *Stand* featured as part of the 2025 National Day of Prayer. To artist Julie Ann Scott for connecting my writing to the Day of Prayer. I thank my official editors, Deb Keiser, Pam Pugh, Brandi Davis, and Bethany Haley, whose names fittingly mean honeybee, honey, wine, and house of figs, for your roles in helping this work cross out of the wilderness and into the "promised land." I am grateful for the creative minds of Mark Ford, Samantha Frolich, Georgie Patt, Aaron Tesauro, and the Vitamin D team who have come around me in this work. To my many unofficial editors, my dear friends, and fellow BECOMERS who have encouraged me in word and deed, from reading chapters and giving critical feedback to hearing my heart and helping me sort my thoughts along the way, I bless you! You have been an excellent and living example of the "Neighborhood Team Effect," both in the storms and in the waiting for this story to be shared.

I am eternally grateful to my mom, dad, brothers, and extended family members who have chosen to follow the Lord and with whom I have been able to safely "cross-tie" in the storms we have weathered together. To my children, Cole, Maya, Leah, and Annika, for your pure-hearted encouragement, unceasing prayers, and genuine sacrifices in these years of writing. To my cousin Jody Olympia, my daily sojourner in this extended writing and editing process —though you claim to be no more than the taxi driver who caught "the baby" on the way to the hospital, I struggle to believe this would have seen the light of day without you and Scott. And to my beloved, Scott, I knew when we married that you would be someone who would STAND with me through life's trials and tribulations. You most certainly have. I praise the Lord for all of you!